Parting Words.

A DISCOURSE

DELIVERED IN THE

NORTH CHURCH, HARTFORD,

JULY 3, 1859.

BY HORACE BUSHNELL.

PUBLISHED BY REQUEST.

HARTFORD:
PUBLISHED BY L. E. HUNT.
1859.

SERMON.

Jer. 22 : 10.—Weep not for the dead, neither bemoan him: but weep sore for him that goeth away; for he shall return no more, nor see his native country.

Weep not for the dead—this man is to be worse than dead, alive without the chance to live; plucked from his throne and carried away, as a prisoner of war, into Egypt, never to return. Challenging sad condolence for him, the tender-hearted prophet raises the figure of a state funeral; the bemoaning cries of the women continued for eight days, the barefoot procession and the cloud of ashes in which it moves, the sad wail of the musicians, and the loud plaint of the people—"Alas! alas! the king!" Not this, he says, but more. Weep not for the dead, neither bemoan him; but weep sore for him that goeth away; for he shall return no more, nor see his native country. Were he only to die and be buried, it would be a case to justify no such bewailing for him, as the heavy years of exile he is to see, his pinings and bitter regrets, his aching hopes and longings never to be fulfilled, his remembrances of a throne first vacant, then occupied by his brother, and he himself a forgotten captive, lost to himself and his country. The sentiment, then, of the prophet is this:—That the trial of being separated from the places and friends grown dear by a customary love is greater, in many respects, than to be separated by death.

He affirms it even of a bad man, though not that it will be, of course, his sentiment. He is such a man as may well enough be much afraid to die, and he may naturally hope that he will somehow be restored to his country and throne. It is only the prophet's own sentiment, knowing that he will not. Far more clear were the truth of it, if he were a good man, consciously ready to die. He could well enough go home to God; but to be separated from the acquaintances, and scenes, and works, in which he has lived, without going home, is a very different matter. He loses the mortal state, without gaining the immortal; goes away alive into exile from his own life itself, the associations it has constructed, the works it has done, the sympathies it has attracted, the very seeds it has planted and fondly hopes to see in their growth.

In tracing briefly the truth of this sentiment, far be it from us to speak lightly of death. To close one's eyes on all that is earthly, to sunder all the ties of mortal love, to wind up the grand affair of trial that we call life, and enter on the fixed result of it, makes the point of death a center where so many mountain-like thoughts crowd heavily in, that we may not think of it as being otherwise than a most trying ordeal to pass. We are only to see that there may be a separation more trying even than this.

And it occurs to us, first of all, that the state of prolonged separation from home, kindred, country, or any place and work where our hearts have learned to find their sphere of enjoyment, is itself a kind of prolonged death. Life unsphered is about the heaviest load ever put upon a mortal. Weariness in a good cause, sacrifice, conflict, are themselves a kind of joy, and, when supported by hope, are often the highest, noblest kind of joy. But to have no place, to have lost a field of customary love and duty, is only to have died before the time; to have died while yet alive; to have all the longings and dear affinities of a living heart, without the work to be done, and the co-operating love and sympathy of such as a good work may attract.

Then, again, the real death itself is still to come—only at a later point; that is, after the living death of exile and a heart unsphered has worn out what remains of the vital energy. And the death it will be, when it comes, as of one cast away upon some desert island—the death of a man out of place, and, as respects the genuine associations and affinities of his position, homeless. He dies touching nobody, and without the sense of being touched by any that have learned to be tenderly regardful of him, unless it be some nearest family friends. If he dies in old age, it is death to nobody but himself, and he drops into the dark river in a kind of unheeded cessation, as a chip drops into the sea.

Again, there is even something inspiring and bright in the death of a faithful and true servant of God, who dies in his place. It is the hour of his reward and crown, and the smile of God's approbation is visibly on him. A kind of halo rests upon the scene. The faces of blessing that crowd about him, and the tender words and ministries in which so many loving affections just now culminate, assure the departing man, and help him in the confidence of victory. Hitherto he has been fighting his cause with many, or, at least, some misgivings. Now, assured by so many witnesses, he dares to sing—"I have fought the good fight, I have finished my course;" and so goes forth to take the crown of glory laid up for him. Exactly contrary is the feeling most natural, where one's roots are torn up and he is driven away alive by the compulsion of Providence. He questions why it is, doubts whether he shall take it as the sentence of God on his defects of duty, struggles heavily with dark accusations of blame, loses the confidence of victory, and finally dies out, coffined, as it were, before the time, in his own seediness and the dullness of his by-gone life. In such a death there may be a true crown, but it does not appear.

Again, it is another kind of contrast, that when one dies in place, in the society where he has lived and the works that have engaged him, his faults are soon forgotten, or quite smoothed away; for we do not like to think ill of the dead, we prefer to cherish only what we have loved or respected. But one who is parted alive from the scenes and works of his life, commonly fares differently. He is found to have been less necessary than many thought. It becomes a kind of surprise that he seemed to be necessary at all. His faults and defects come up to account for the discovery. And, being still alive, he is obliged to know that he is gone by—not forgotten, not disrespected, it may be, but desired with less warmth and practically held in terms of qualified estimation. Probably no one is to be blamed on this account. It is simply human that it should be so, and it can not be otherwise.

There is yet another mode in which the living man, separated from his work, is often made to suffer in feeling more unjustly. Whatever miscarriages, failures, faultinesses may appear, after he is gone, will be too easily set down as effects of his mistaken ways and methods. Men are easily wise in tracing effects to remote causes, and they sometimes quite as easily find a subtle personal interest of self-excusing in it. And this is the more likely to happen in the case of a Christian teacher, benefactor, founder, reformer, that the very fruits, all the fruits he leaves behind, being such as pertain to human character, are themselves unripe, imperfect, planted thick with all manner of bad seeds ready to grow apace, when opportunity is given. Had he remained, such growth might have been kept under. But they sprout into rank luxuriance, it may be, after he is gone, overgrowing the field with thorns and briars. And then how easily is he shown to be the responsible cause. And there is no defence to be made. Were he dead and entered into rest with God, such accusations, even if they were known to him, would not trouble him. But he lives to hear of them in his exile, having all his human weaknesses upon him, and quite broken down, it may be, under them. Dead while yet living, he is overtaken by a judgment-day sentence on his works, from which there is no appeal, though it be cruelly untrue. Heavy is the load that many good men, fondly loved in their time, have been called to bear, in the last days of life, under this very common, always possible, injustice. Not to have some rational forecast of it, would argue even dullness and a short perception of mankind.

It is hardly necessary in adjusting the contrast of death and a living separation, to dwell on the two translations themselves,—one to a condition of fulness, rest, divine approbation, glorified society, brightness and peace eternal; the other to a state of living exile and emptiness, where the roots strike down no more; where the work is ended without being finished; where the mind struggles vainly after what it has lost, and has little hope of anything further to be gained; where friends are gratuities and not rights, politely deferent or considerate, but as late comers, easily considerate of themselves; where, in short, the unsphered man is only put in schooling, under a last lesson of loss and emptiness, for the great release to come.

I will not dwell on the comparison longer. You will only observe that all these considerations have a greatly augmented force, when applied to the removal of a Christian minister from his flock, after many years of watch and service among them. He is knit to them by the working habit of his life itself. I will not assume that he is less selfish in his work than other men are in theirs. Still it is much that the form of it is such as to make them his object, and set all the forces of his nature running after them and their personal benefit. If he kindles in it, he kindles for them. If he struggles heavily and wearily, they are the burden he carries. If he succeeds, the success is in them. He looks on them as having all his life-work in them, and they become, in that manner, the native country of his heart. And this will be true if he is only not more selfish than other men. The formal aim of his work is such as to concentrate even his mixed motives and keep them generating a kind of love; which, if it be doubtfully Christian, is yet intensely personal. Thus, while other men are localized in their attachments by the accident of birth, or pleasant associations, or by long residence, he is drilling even a flinty nature, it may be, under the hammer of work, and setting in clamps of attachment that fasten him to his flock and sphere. Whatever genuinely Christian love, too, there was in him is fanned to a flame by the whole stress of his endeavor, made personal towards them and fastened upon them, by a grasp that has eternity in it; even as it is their perilous eternity that he has been laboring to rescue and glorify by the grace of an eternal salvation. If, mean time, he is happy enough to gain their personal love to himself, it is a most honest, real kind of love; love that has grown up in a dealing with their faults and a purging of their sins, love that comes back, wafting heavenly flavors on him, out of their new eternity in Christ already begun. His faults they have gladly buried even before the time. They have borne him up in his weaknesses, sheltered him, it may be, in his storms, and have so become a kind of complementary force to his life. He scarce knows how to be himself, separated from them. The natural and proper close of his connexion would be, just here, to let him die, and sleep with their dead. "Weep sore" for him, if it must be otherwise.

Otherwise alas! it is to be with me. The hand of God is upon me and I must go. I have struggled long with this dark necessity, and you on your part have also detained me. Were I dislodged by you, I should probably go with greater pains and fewer regrets. It is even a part of my happiness that I can go with these regrets upon me. They are heavy enough indeed, to create a pain, but the pain were much heavier without them. I perceive as distinctly beforehand, as I can at any future time, that when I am finally separated from this dear flock, who have been the home of my heart for so many years, I shall be sick, and weary, and look back with longings not to be suppressed, on these pastorly works and cares, these answering words and faces, left behind. It is the reward of a christian minister, if successful, that he becomes the object of a wide affection. The business man, the lawyer, and even the physician, commonly has his work as work, and gets his affectional interest mostly in his family and among his small circle of friends. But the happy minister lives in a great family affection, and it bye and bye becomes a kind of necessity. He grows into it, feeds upon it, and the separation from it makes a fearful desolation. I go in the definite understanding that I am never to be so insphered again; for my life is too far spent, and my constitution too much damaged, to allow the hope that I can ever take the charge of another pulpit and people. And, if it were otherwise, none but a young man ever can be thoroughly inserted into any people's love. One of the great faults of my ministry among you has been, that I have had too little consideration of what was due to my own self-preservation, and so I have spent the robustness of a naturally long lived force, before the time. Acknowledging the wrong, I am ready also to accept the penalty. You have kindly urged me to stay with you, and you have generously offered to have me as a burden, when you could not have me any longer as an effective pastor and servant. You have even claimed it as your right, to repay, in this manner, what you have generously agreed to consider a debt, fairly incurred. But the sense of being a burden and living as a pensioner, you can readily see, might, to persons of a certain temperament, be insupportable. I acknowledge it is so to me; not because I distrust your constancy in such pledges, but because it involves the being consciously a drawback on your prosperity as a congregation, which it has been the habitual study of my life to advance. Your interest plainly requires me to be gone, and obediently to that I go. Rational convictions must, in such a matter, take the lead of personal inclinations, and must rule down even the protest of the mutinous affections. You must have a minister who can actively serve you. To him you must give your hearts, undivided, undetained, by recollections or regrets that look towards another who only could, but cannot effectively, serve you, longer. Let the field be his, as the work must be, and let all your affections and prayers cluster faithfully and singly round him.

I ought perhaps to say that it is not merely to gain a lengthened lease of life that I am induced to make this trying sacrifice. If I had nothing to live for, I certainly would not wish to live a day longer. But I am encouraged in the hope of being so far recovered in health, that I may prosecute, in a careful way, objects and themes of study that appear to me to have no secondary importance. I hope to support a fractional ministry by the press, when I cannot the full routine of the pastoral office. In this hope I consent to go into exile, though to sever these ties and tear myself away costs me a struggle which I will not trust myself to describe; a struggle which I try to compose by indulging the further hope, that I may yet return to Hartford and here may close my days. My dear people I cannot have again—they are mine no more—but it will be something, if I may, to die among them, and be finally lodged, as a resurrection guest, in the dust of a city whose people I have loved the more, that I have tried to serve them, and have experienced, at their hands, so much of confidence, good will and forbearance.

I suppose I could speak here, if I would, of some advances made and fruits gathered; for I certainly think that my ministry has not been altogether useless. But I am not in any mood of boasting, or even of self-gratulation. I am under the rod, where it much better sorts with my feeling to be dumb. If any good has been done, refer it wholly to God; if any loss suffered, who shall take the blame if not I? Any smallest recollection of success is just now an offence to me. My heart runs not that way—let me hasten my escape from the windy storm and tempest. If by some statistical review, or comparison, it might be shown that I found you weak, and now leave you strong, what but just this same increase ought the growth of your city itself to have yielded, under the most indifferent kind of ministry? Or if we make up the count of such as have been born here, how often has that God whose prerogative it is to bring water out of rock, shown a much longer train of converts, marching out heavenward, from under a secretly, and afterwards publicly, apostate ministry! No! God forbid that in this life-time funeral, I should think to while away the pains of it by any pleasant computations of results. I see little now but my personal faults and the faults of my preaching. What! such a gospel as this! gospel of salvation to lost men! gospel of the manifested love of God in Christ's dear life and passion! such a gospel, preached so feebly, with so little unction of love, and with so many mixed motives present to mar the effect—I have no heart to think of any pleasant congratulations in it! Forgive it, O my God, and I ask no more!

And yet I ought to thank God that the result has not been worse. Nay, I ought to thank him for a kind of paradoxical happiness continued to me in a ministry so defective. I have generally had a great and sometimes even a superlative enjoyment, in just that which now, in the review, appears to me to have been so far below the real import of my work. Had I another life to spend, with talents high enough to command any highest post of honor in the world, I would hasten straight into this ministry of Jesus, if it were only for the sublime enjoyment of being unfolded in such themes and such ranges of feeling and work. I would only try to be faithful and single enough in the calling to be allowed to die in it.

I would count it too as my happiness to be located in this same church, in this same city of Hartford. Not because you are any but a sinful people. But it makes a great difference what kind of sinful people one has given him to do his work upon. If they were not in sin, they would want no ministry; if they were as ungenerously and coarsely tempered in it as many are, they would scarce be able to receive one. I found you not homogeneous. You had many jealousies. I encountered some of them. But if there were some of you that were unreasonable for a time, there were none that wished to hinder the truth, none that did not so far honor the gospel as to want their benefit in it, and moderate their manners by the gracious spirit of it. No properly factious man have I ever found among you. And it has been my happiness to see you gradually flowing towards a complete unity. You have allowed me to speak plainly, as I now think, sometimes over-severely, of your sins. My preaching, for a time, was too much in that vein. But my entire freedom of utterance you have never restrained. You have even supported me in it, in times of bitter impeachment from without; standing with me, unable to be moved or swerved in your confidence by public combinations of protest and offended authority pressing down upon you for years. And you were not blind in this confidence. Only your convictions were different from the convictions of those who had less opportunity, and, it may be, less carefulness, to know; and you have it for your reward that they are just now discovering yours to have been right—right not simply as being righteous, but doubly and nobly right that, as righteous men, you were able to stand fast in them. Any three of your number, shaken loose by these assaults, could have instituted charges against me that would have put me in the power of my adversaries at once; but no first one of that three could be found.

Out of such an experience of you, my confidence grew apace. And as confidence begets love, and love begets returning love, we have grown together in a kind of conjugal understanding and felt community of life and character, such as seldom is known in the happiest of pastoral relations. With you thus for twenty-six years, in all the tenderest issues and subtlest windings of your life; by you in your disasters and troubles, and in your holidays of success; close enough to you to feel the touch of your anxieties and tremblings for your children, and the throb of your private thanksgivings on account of them; at your weddings, by you in your sick chambers and your funerals, with you in your struggles under, and with, and out of your sins, sometimes crossing you a little, and sometimes a little crossed by you—with no other effect than that pulling the cord has tightened it—in this manner my ministry among you has been a kind of course in trust and well experimented affection, a good element for courage and growth, an element, at once, of stimulus and rest for the heart. No minister of Christ was ever more happy in his people, and I hasten to acknowledge the favor, not so much for your sakes, as because my consciousness of desert before God is just now humbled to a point so far below the conditions of privilege allowed me. I have never been willing, I most certainly know, to swerve you, even by a hair's breadth, from the truth. I have been religiously careful to correct myself into and by the truth; allowing no small fear of man, or smaller pride of consistency, to detain me. I know that I have loved the truth. But I ought to have made the truth much greater, more nearly indentical with God, closer to love; so, more savingly powerful in you, more captivatingly, gloriously sovereign over you. Truth has her due honors, not when she is thought or reasoned, but when she reigns. Truth is the mother of salvation, and her word is fitly preached, only when her saving motherhood is proved in the spiritual birth and gathering of her children. And here it is that I seem to have come short of my privilege. I probably could not be satisfied here, indeed I ought not to be satisfied, as long as any that have heard me with approval are left unprofited by me.

How many things crowd upon me now, at such an hour as this, which I could wish to press upon you, for your future benefit and growth. Pardon me, if then,

I proceed to name a few articles of advice suggested by my deep concern for your welfare.

Have it then as a great point of duty, never to be remitted, that you maintain a christian care of your families. A christian Church and Sunday are not enough; you must have a christian week, and house, and home, a genuinely christian nurture for your children. What I have so often urged on this point has been growing into a stronger and more fixed conviction even to this hour; that it is your privilege, and, being your privilege, your most sacred duty, to see your children grow up into Christ as children of grace, and born of the Spirit, even before the time of their definite recollection. But, in order to this, you must make a christian element of the house. And what can do more for you, as respects the godly keeping of your lives, than to heartily accept and carefully cherish this responsibility? What, again, more for the solid prosperity of religion in your church, than to have your character and that of your children grounded in a mode of life so practically christian?

You are soon to have a minister, I trust, in my place. Let it be his fault, not yours, if he does not succeed. Anticipate his wants, as you have anticipated mine. Show him the same kindness and forbearance you have shown to me. Gather round him in the same stedfast affection. Guarantee his liberty by the same generous confidence and support. As he is one and you are many, understand that he is weak alone, and without the hearty co-operation of your works and prayers. Let his words have a warm place to fall in, and commend them to others by a faithful practice in yourselves.

Have it also as another point of duty, to provide all

the equipments necessary to success, and to make a liberal expenditure for it. A christian spirit without public spirit is simply absurd, and this, to you, is happily no discovery. You have undertaken to build a church, in a location better adapted to your present places of residence. That church, as you well understand, must be built. It will never do for a thrifty cause to faint, or recede; what is attempted must be done; vigorously, triumphantly done. As nothing but this same undertaking could before save you and make your way to prosper, so, now that you have made a beginning, a double necessity is on you. There is no society weakness so weak, so impossible even to live, as that which has the consciousness of breaking down. You have not come to this, and I have a most assured confidence that you never will. It has been well for you to be deliberate and cautious; to be slack and faint hearted has never been your manner, and you must be greatly altered before it can be.

In the matter of christian truth and doctrine, understand that your responsibilities are as great as the sacred interests of a gospel for the world's salvation require them to be.. Hitherto you have been mainly concerned to assert a larger liberty and a more generous, more comprehensive, doctrine. But the time may come, as I may not have sufficiently warned you, when you will be called to set yourselves, with as great firmness, against the encroachments of a destructive and vapid liberalism. Offer no least allowance to any real departure from truth. Standing for no one form or formulary as a law by which to measure and condemn all others, have it as a point of honor, even, squarely to reject as christian, whoever really rejects the Christ in whom you trust. Assert, above all, and stand by the assertion of, a supernatural gospel; for there is, in fact, no other, and whoever scorns or only disowns such a gospel, let him be to you as a heathen man and a publican,—deist, pantheist, atheist, or pagan, but no christian. Studying always breadth of doctrine, which is the manner of God's word itself, make that study safe, by presenting a front of rock to all the prurient forms of error that human shallowness and conceit may gender, under the pretext of liberty. There is a kind of breadth that would make you a superficies only and no substance—that is not for you.

It will be a great point with you also to maintain unity among yourselves. Truth flies every place where the noise of strife is heard. How can the body prosper, when the members tear each other. In this fact of unity, you have had your strength even from the earliest day of my connexion with you. And you are mortgaged to it now, as I believe, by a more felt conviction than ever. Temporary jars and frictions of disagreement will appear among brethren, as they did among the apostles themselves; but they will never grow to factions and fixed animosities. When society breaks in this manner, it is even a low sign; showing that irresponsible talkers, ready and rank haters, fomentors of idle jealousies, and other such fire-brand characters, are the coarse material of which it is made. Society supposes a character of public reason, consideration for it, deference and concession to it, and a capacity of many-sided care and generous allowance to preserve it; and it, in turn, gives dignity to all the members, because it trains them in a voluntary moderation of their passions, caprices and asperities. Christian society, therefore, well maintained, bears the highest character of dignity, because it is closest, comprehends things deepest in feeling and thought, and requires the firmest self-moderation, the tenderest forbearance, the widest charity, and the noblest sacrifice and devotion to a common cause. Here is your best strength, in this only can you stand.

I will not multiply these points of advice; for there are one or two matters of concern more tender than these, where I must be allowed, in closing, to draw myself closer to your feeling. I have spoken of your great kindness and your unwonted fidelity to me, as a pastor, in my whole ministry among you. But in closing up this ministry, my heart turns with even the greater sorrow, to many, who have given no evidence, either to themselves or to me, that they have received any saving profit in it. You are all my friends and have heard me, these many years, in no unfriendly manner. I readily admit that, having so great advantage, I ought to have left a much smaller number behind me unreconciled to God; and yet I must believe that a most serious charge of blame is resting with you; for you certainly could have been thus reconciled. Many times have you inwardly approved and deeply felt the message I have brought you. I doubt not that to yourselves even, you have seemed to be powerfully drawn by the appeals of the great salvation, feebly presented and blameably defective in urgency, as I now see them to have been. You felt the argument, your immortal convictions were deeply moved, the sublime wants and longings of your spiritual nature were set a hungering after God, Christ and the cross, melted lovingly into your feeling; and yet you did not come. You said with the Athenian judges addressed by Paul, and strangely impressed by his words, "we will hear thee again of this matter." And so you have continued, some of you till your heads are silvering with grey, baffling the gospel even by the play of your sensibilities under it, and removing both it and your salvation farther off, by your very approvals of the truth; saying always, "We will hear thee again, the word is good, the subject is great and true, we will hear thee again of this matter." Hear thee again! No, the end is now come. This day's sermon is the last of my ministry with you; the really sad thing to me is, that my experiment with you is ended. I look back on you now, as a ship looks back on the receding shore. I am not permitted to think that my long ministry with you has done you any good, and now it is close upon just the last moment of it. No affectation is it, when I say, that my heart aches with a double regret; for myself that I have preached a gospel to you,—power of God though it be—having still so little power; for you that you have turned away from such as you have had. Give me then the privilege of one more appeal and that the very last. You did not expect, I know, when you came to hear this farewell sermon, that it was to be anything more than a leave-taking. But how can it be truly that, unless it closes up our relation in some way fitting to the close? Shall it be the silent, barren close of a final and fixed negation of good, in all that I have sought, and taught, and preached, and prayed, for you, in this ministry of so many years? Have you entertained it so kindly, waited on it so assentingly, to conclude in the discovery that you have wholly and finally rejected it, and Christ himself commended to you by it? With such an issue, has not this ministry been a most sad experiment for you? Might you not well be startled by the result of it? Is it vain to ask that you will make this eleventh hour, last hour as it is, the hour of your sealing? Pass it now as your fixed resolve, that what you have so long approved shall close in benefit; that here, to-day, you will begin a christian life; that my testimony for Christ shall not be finished as a rejected testimony. Remember the parable Christ has so kindly given to encourage and assure you in this late coming. Such a resolve, honestly taken, and followed by all due application to God for help, though prepared by no previous agitations of thought, or struggles of feeling, he will assuredly approve and will issue it for you speedily in all the evidences you can desire. Then the sad necessity is no more on me; I can meet you then, as I shortly must, before my judge and yours, not as rejecters, but as doers of the word, and heirs of Christ, coming joyfully in, to remember the grace of this last, eleventh hour call of my otherwise profitless and guilt-increasing ministry.

In looking over my work and its results, I encounter also another and different kind of regret, which relates, my dear brethren in Christ, to you. I name it not that I may lay reproof upon you in this closing hour, but that I may give you, in such plainness, a fit proof of my enduring and faithfully christian regard. I regret no special deficiencies in you, as compared with other disciples of our time. My complaint would rather be that, if you are somewhat raised, you are yet too little raised above their pitch or standard. For it is to me a fact most deplorable, that the christian disciples of our time appear to know so little of Christ, and rest in conceptions of the christian grace so restricted—serving legally, and calling it '*service*' to be christian; conscientious, but not free; holding well the observances, but not walking joyfully in them; doing certain works and offering certain contributions in the name of a benevolence, but not embarked and floated in the bliss of love; looking mainly to condition still for happiness, to property, society, show, and habitually running after these as the main reliances and best goods of life; showing, in this manner, how small is the Christ they believe in—small exactly as the space he fills. I wanted, my brethren, to have brought you on a great way farther, and it affects me with deep sorrow, in just this view, that I have preached Christ to you for so long a time, and yet have given to so few, to really know the fullness and world-diminishing glory of Jesus in the heart—the close acquaintance, the immediate manifestation, the liberty, the peace, the riches, the lifted consciousness, the sublime equilibrium of joy, the all-conquering bliss of endurance.

I should be still more oppressed in feeling, if I could not believe that you have made advances, and some of you great advances, on the average piety of the times. When I see, as I just now am allowed to see, how speedily the grace of Christ that is in you, hid for a few days by the smoke of a disturbed feeling raised inadvertently and by surprise, struggles up into clear ascendancy, I thank God for the sign. It shows the love-grace of Jesus to be powerful enough in you to resume its sway, at once, just where commonly nothing but a long run of time and a final wearing out of passion is able to restore equilibrium. But accepting this gladly as a special evidence for you, I am yet partial enough in my concern to be not wholly satisfied.

For a time has come when they that stand for Christ must be either a great deal better in their life, or else a great deal worse. All the fiery woes of persecution that, in former ages, burnt in a saintly piety, are extinguished. The way to heaven is grown easy and safe, under the guarantee of our modern liberties. The world, meantime, is in a tide of economic progress—the very soil of the world is being scientifically fattened for a more copious production. Wealth is becoming, thus, a hope more nearly universal, and so, luxury, show, fashion, are becoming a kind of general ambition. A great and fearful problem is thus raised for the gospel: how to let in riches into piety itself; how to make a solid union between power and humility; how to raise the tastes and manners, and keep the simplicity of feeling; how to amplify conditions, without raising puffs and swells in the men; in one word, how to bring in means, and not bring dissipations, fumings of pride, vapors of conceit, shows of vanity, apings of the great world of ungodliness. Such a fool is man that, getting power, he loses sobriety; and it is yet to be seen whether even the lowly-minded, self-renouncing religion of Jesus can save a prospering age from this folly. What is specially wanted therefore now is christian men and churches who maintain the open state with God; living joyfully above the world, when the world's best gifts are theirs; godly, self-renouncing, simple, responsible, using their great means for great benefactions, and finding always, in the riches of Christ, a heaven-full of consciously ennobled joy and peace, such as plainly no inferior good can yield. What we want is christian men and families who can be saints without being persecuted or poor; men who, having mastered all prosperity, can master also themselves; who, having conquered all the good of time, can conquer it again by being superior to it; doing honor to God's abounding fatherhood in all most generous uses of his gifts, and yet in such a way, all ascetic practices apart, that not his gifts but He Himself will ever be the joy, and rest, and fullness of their heart. The low, legal, anxious piety now commonly prevalent is far too doubtfully blessed in Christ—a kind of starvation, out of which the soul hies herself eagerly to lay hold of almost any sort of good. It is no argument for unworldliness, but the greatest temptation to it rather. Nothing answers now but fullness in Christ, riches above all riches, glory within above all glories without, to be imparadised in faith, and God to faith revealed.

This high summit, my brethren, I have endeavored to clear to you so that you could see it. I have shown it to be not too high—to be in fact the real original Christianity. The doctrine of low living and all the underbrush of false sanctimony by which the truth is hid, I have carefully cut away. This it is, I have shown you, to be christian—this, and nothing less; to be joyful in Christ and free; to know God consciously; to live an inspired life, clean above the world and even above yourself. Would that I could leave you in a more certain confidence that you are all entered into this path and walking in this grace. It would fill me with unspeakable sorrow, if I thought you had fallen away from it by any fault of mine. I shall long to hear of your affairs and how you do in this very thing. For it is a matter of comparatively trivial consequence whether you get a small man for your minister, or a great; whether your house is thinly attended or crowded by eager multitudes. The first and chief matter is that your conversation is in heaven; that you live unworldly lives and give an example to men of the abounding fullness and joy to be found in Christ Jesus your Lord. In this I shall ever long after you and circumvent you with my continual prayers.

But I must desist. The dreaded hour has come, and I must go. These scenes of duty that have been my enjoyment, these familiar faces, responsive always to my words, and works, and prayers—from these I must tear myself away alive, as I was just now saying, and take the separation, more trying than to die, for my lot. I go not out, as I trust, from the presence of the Lord, but my work with you is done, and from you I must now be parted. Before God I thank you for your patience with my defects, and the unwonted kindness you have shown me. I shall still be watching for you in deep pastorly feeling, though pastor no more. If it is laid upon me to die in parts remote, I shall not go as one quite separated from you, but shall go looking to a blessed reunion with your friends and mine—dear, blessed names that I could not pronounce without tears and a faltering voice—now bright and spotless in glory before God, accepted of Jesus and dear to him, in eternal companionship, as to us. Thither too arriving, if by grace I am able, I shall also be looking after you and waiting for your coming. Pardon me also if I try to hope it may then be discovered that I have done you more good than I thought, and have won a greater property in you than I feared.

Till that day I commit you, one and all, to the tender keeping of our common Lord and Saviour. The grace of our Lord Jesus Christ be with you all—in this, Farewell.

www.ingramcontent.com/pod-product-compliance
Lightning Source LLC
LaVergne TN
LVHW011144110826
845150LV00008B/2503
* 9 7 8 1 4 1 8 1 9 2 7 8 5 *